Roses

Victoria Blakemore

Copyright info/picture credits

Cover, saschanti/AdobeStock; Page 3, LanKS/Shutterstock; Page 5, Couleur/Pixabay; Page 7, nastya_gepp/Pixabay; Page 9, manfredrichter/Pixabay; Page 11, wolfman57/ Shutterstock; Page 13, Evtushkova Olga/Shutterstock; Page 15, MabelAmber/Pixabay; Page 17, Konevi/Pixabay; Page 19, kareni/Pixabay; Page 21, Soupoffun/Pixabay; Page 23; KIM-DAEJEUNG/Pixabay; Page 25, UpPiJ/Pixabay; Page 27, Evan Lorne/Shutterstock; Page 29, Peggychoucair/Pixabay; Page 31, silviarita/Pixabay; Page 33, saschanti/AdobeStock

Table of Contents

What Are Roses?

Roses are a kind of flower. They belong to a family of plants that include apples, strawberries, cherries, peaches, and more.

There are over 150 different kinds of roses. They differ in their color, size, where they grow, and the kind of blooms they have.

Roses are often red, pink, yellow, or white. They can also be colors like purple, orange, or peach.

3

History

Roses are believed to have been first **cultivated** in China over 5,000 years ago. They were soon grown in many parts of the Middle East.

Roses were used by the ancient Romans and the Greek for celebrations, medicine, and perfume.

Hybrid roses were first grown in

the 1860's. They are made by

combining two different kinds

of roses.

5

The Wars of the Roses were fought in England in the 1400's. They got their name from the white and red roses used to **symbolize** each side.

Roses became popular in Europe in the 1800's. Many **botanists** created **hybrid** roses that bloomed longer, had different colors, or larger blooms.

Roses are a very popular flower

for gardens and bouquets.

They are often given as gifts on

occasions like Valentine's Day. 7

Life Cycle

First, a seed is planted in soil. With enough water and **nutrients**, it grows into a sprout. The sprout grows a stem that has leaves and buds.

The buds open up into flowers. Once the flowers have fallen off, the fruits are left behind. The fruits contain the new seeds.

Roses are **perennial** flowers. This means that they can grow and flower for many years.

Seeds

In order to grow a rose plant from seeds, they need to be prepared first. This is done by putting seeds in damp soil and storing them somewhere cold.

After a few weeks, the seeds can be taken out of the cold. Then, they should start to sprout and are ready to be planted.

The rose hips are the fruit of the rose plant. They are left on the stem after the flowers fall off.

Roots

The roots grow from the seeds. They grow downward into the soil and help to **anchor** the plant. They keep it in place as it grows.

The roots take in water and **nutrients** from the soil. These **nutrients** help the plant to grow and stay healthy.

Cuttings taken from rose bushes can be planted in soil. They can grow roots after they are planted.

Stems

Rose stems are hard and thick. They grow upwards from the seeds. The stems help the plant to stand up. The leaves and flowers grow from the stem.

The stem helps to transport water and **nutrients** from the roots to the other parts of the plant.

While they are usually called

thorns, the sharp points that

most roses have on their stems

are actually prickles.

Leaves

Rose leaves grow in **alternating** directions. If one is growing to the left, then the next leaf will grow to the right.

Rose bush leaves have an important job. They make energy from sunlight in a process called **photosynthesis**.

Some rose leaves have sharp

edges. They can also have

sharp prickles underneath.

Flowers

Although we call the colorful part of a rose the flower, the true name is the corolla. It is made up of the colorful petals.

Roses can have anywhere from five to over fifty petals. Their flowers can be single, or one per stem. They can also grow in clusters.

Roses can have several rows of

petals. Roses that have more

rows of petals look fuller.

Pollination

When pollen from a flower is moved to a new flower, the new flower has been pollinated. Flowers that have been pollinated can make fruit and seeds.

The wind can blow pollen from one flower to another. Animals can also spread pollen.

Pollinators such as bees collect

pollen from roses. When they fly

to different flowers, they spread

the pollen.

Where Are Roses Grown?

Ecuador grows and sells more roses than any other country. Colombia, Ethiopia, Kenya, and India also grow and sell many roses.

Roses often grow best in warm places. Only a few kinds of roses can survive in places with very cold winters.

Most roses bloom in the spring

or summer. Some kinds of roses

bloom twice each year.

Celebrating Roses

Many flower festivals that celebrate roses are held around the world.

One famous event is the annual Rose Parade in California. Large floats are designed and covered with roses of all different colors.

Parades around the world

feature floats that are decorated

with roses and other flowers.

Eating Roses

Rose petals and rose hips are both **edible**. They are safe to eat. Rose petals are sometimes used as a **garnish**. They can add flavor and color to a meal.

Rose hips are a fruit and can be eaten on their own. They are also used to make tea, jelly, syrup, sauces, and soups.

Rose petal jam is a popular way to use rose petals in food. It is sweet and can be spread on bread or muffins.

Nutrition

Rose petals are mostly made of water, so they are very low in calories. They do have a small amount of vitamin C.

Rose hips are higher in vitamin C. They also contain some vitamin K, E, and A. These vitamins can help you to have healthy skin, blood, and eyes.

The vitamins found in rose hips

can also help to keep you from

getting sick.

Other Uses

Rose petals can be used to make rose water or rose oil. The **antioxidants** found in rose water can help to keep our body healthy.

When put on the skin, rose water can help to soothe irritation. It can also be used to help treat cuts and burns.

Roses have a sweet **fragrance**.

They are often used in

perfumes or beauty products.

Symbolism

Flowers are often used to **symbolize** different ideas and feelings. Roses are often used to symbolize love.

Different colors of roses stand for different things. Red roses **symbolize** love. Yellow roses are thought to stand for friendship.

Pink roses can be used to **symbolize** gratitude, joy, or admiration.

Glossary

Alternating: following each other in turns, first one side, then the other

Anchor: to keep stable or in place

Antioxidant: a substance that can help to repair some damage in our cells

Botanist: someone who studies plants

Combining: putting together

Cultivated: when a plant is planted on purpose and helped to grow

Cutting: a part of a plant that has been cut from a grown plant so it can be planted

Edible: safe to eat

Fragrance: a nice smell

Garnish: something that is used to add flavor, color, or texture to food

Hybrid: the offspring of two plants or animals that are different species

Nutrient: something that helps people, plants, or animals to grow

Occasion: a special event

Perennial: a plant that lives longer than two years

Photosynthesis: the process a plant uses to make sunlight into energy

Pollinator: something that carries pollen to a plant

Symbolize: to represent or stand for something

About the Author

Victoria Blakemore is a first grade

teacher in Southwest Florida with a

passion for reading.

You can visit her at

www.elementaryexplorers.com

Also in This Series

Gray Wolves	Sloths	Flamingos	Camels	Koalas	Honey Bees	Pandas
Pangolins	White-Tailed Deer	Orcas	Giraffes	Corn	Meerkats	Echidnas
Walruses	Raccoons	Bald Eagles	Apples	Arctic Foxes	Red Pandas	Cassowaries
Tigers	Ladybugs	Moose	Beluga Whales	Leopards	Elephants	Jellyfish
Binturongs	Lions	Dolphins	Reindeer	Hammerhead Sharks	Hippos	Pumpkins
Peafowl	Chameleons	Florida Panthers	Aye-Ayes	Black Bears	Cheetahs	Manatees
Gingerbread	Polar Bears	Hot Chocolate	Orangutans	Coyotes	Marshmallows	Strawberries

Victoria Blakemore

Also in This Series

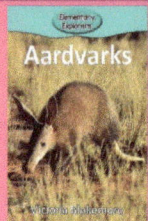

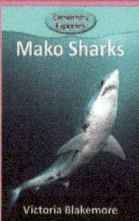

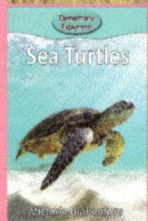

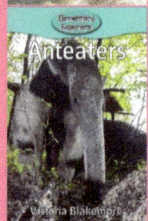

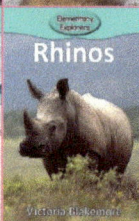

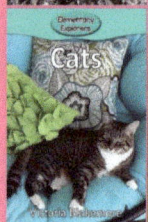

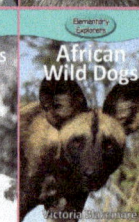

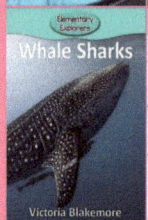

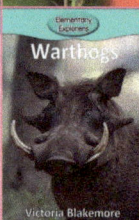

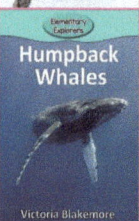

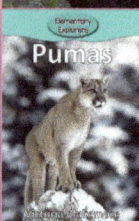

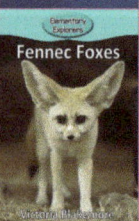

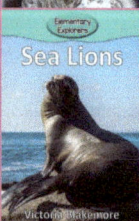

Aardvarks	Mako Sharks	Alligators	Frogs	Hedgehogs	Brown Bears	Bongos
Sea Turtles	Quokkas	Muskrats	Zebras	Red Foxes	Ring-Tailed Lemurs	Platypuses
Anteaters	Kangaroos	Rhinos	Jaguars	Wombats	Capybaras	Gorillas
Cats	Skunks	Butterflies	Dingoes	Snow Leopards	African Wild Dogs	Penguins
Whale Sharks	Wolverines	Warthogs	Caracals	Badgers	Seals	Hummingbirds
Pikas	Humpback Whales	Pumas	Lemonade	Llamas	Tulips	Ostriches
Sunflowers	Fennec Foxes	Sea Lions	Squirrels	Roses		

All titles by Victoria Blakemore (Elementary Explorers)

www.ingramcontent.com/pod-product-compliance
Lightning Source LLC
Chambersburg PA
CBHW051253020426
42333CB00025B/3193